12 PO......

PRINCIPLES OF
PROSPEROUS
LAW PRACTICES

BY **RICHARD JACOBS** & **TRACY MERDA**

Speakeasy Marketing, Inc.

73-03 Bell Blvd, #10

Oakland Gardens, NY 11364

(888) 225-8594

www.SpeakeasyMarketingInc.com

Ordering Information:

Quantity sales. Special discounts are available on quantity purchases by corporations, associations, and others. For details, contact the publisher at the address above.

Orders by U.S. trade bookstores and wholesalers. Please contact Speakeasy Marketing: Tel: **(888)** 225-8594 or visit www.SpeakeasyMarketingInc.com.

Printed in the United States of America

Published in 2020

ISBN: 978-1-951149-33-8

DEDICATION

This book is dedicated to the solo and small law firms I've worked with, and the ones I have yet to work with. As you discover the world of marketing, sales, and great customer service, it's my hope that the principles espoused by the "greats" in these industries guide you towards a successful and fulfilling practice for many years to come.

Practicing law is a noble profession (although I have never done so), and I have the honor and privilege of having helped over 1,000 attorneys these past 11 years.

As I hone my craft, may you hone yours. As I discover the most powerful principles that TRULY lead to success in business, may you read them in these pages and yourself, prosper by them.

ACKNOWLEDGEMENTS

My co-author, Tracy Merda, has become a powerhouse in her own right, and now leads Speakeasy's publishing arm for ambitious professionals.

Tracy makes me look like a disorganized klutz in comparison. She handles more clients, in a professional, dignified and expert way than I ever could on my own.

After interviewing well over 700 attorneys the past 4+ years, Tracy's knowledge of the legal profession and the unique challenges attorneys face nationwide has become extensive, deep, and unparalleled.

I'd like to acknowledge her work, assistance, friendship, and expertise in helping Speakeasy to become a tremendous success.

…and helping over 250 attorneys to become first-time authors through our Speak-a-Book process is another great accomplishment. Thanks Tracy!

DISCLAIMER

This publication is intended to be used for educational purposes only. No writer-reader relationship is intended to be created by reading this material. The publisher, authors, and all business associates assume no liability for any errors or omissions or for how this book or its contents are used or interpreted or for any consequences resulting directly or indirectly from the use of this book or the material therein.

If you are an attorney, please know that the material in this book may conflict with local, state or federal bar requirements, ethics requirements for being an attorney, or other requirements or laws. Nothing in this book should be construed to be legal, ethical, or otherwise. Your implementation, reliance on, or use of any of the information contained in this book is at your own risk.

TESTIMONIALS

"Speakeasy Marketing Is The Best Thing That Has Happened To My Law Practice!"

"I can say unequivocally that Speakeasy Marketing is the best thing that has happened to my law practice! I have been a practicing attorney in New Haven, Connecticut for over 36 years and I have tried so many different marketing methods and firms that I can no longer keep track. Often times, I have been a sucker for pitches that over-promised and under-delivered. These experiences made me gun-shy and I was reluctant to build a website and market my practice anymore. However, Richard made a convincing presentation over the telephone and thereafter in person prompting me to give him a chance. Well, as I said earlier, it was career changing! My website is the envy of my colleagues and my practice is thriving at a time when my peers are struggling. Speakeasy's employees are proactive and suggest changes and improvements all of the time and it is only my laziness that keeps me from helping them do more. They are prompt in replying to questions and they are helpful with all matters of technology that I struggle with. I cannot say enough about Richard and his team! I Hope my Speakeasy Marketing Review helps other fellow clients in their professional practice."

— *Jack O'Donnell, Esq.*

****

"Speakeasy Is A Godsend And A Bargain"

"Speakeasy is a godsend and a bargain. I've been through two other marketing companies, but no one was as hands-on as my Speakeasy team are. I've seen other marketing companies who do the same level of services charge as much as $3,000-$4,000 a month, but Speakeasy was very affordable. They gave me a high-quality well-polished website, complete with updated profile photos, social media management, videos, content/articles, and testimonials. As a lawyer and a solo practitioner, they made getting clients easy and took everything off my hands so I could focus on what I do best: being an awesome attorney."

— *Rebecca Royer, Esq.*

****

"My Total Business Income Increased By Approximately $40,000"

"I have been using Speakeasy for approximately one year. In that time period, my total business income increased by approximately $40,000. In that same time period, I also generated enough calls that I was able to limit the cases I took to those in local counties, decreasing my time traveling to and from court. I am very satisfied with their services."

— *Derek R. Ewin, Esq.*

****

"I Especially Appreciate Speakeasy's Common Sense Approach To The Marketing Of Professional Services."

"Speakeasy Marketing designed our website (forbankruptcy.com). We have had websites designed by others over the years. By far, Speakeasy did the best job. It looks very professional and motivates potential clients to call the office. I probably drove them crazy with the many changes I requested and the video I asked to be included in the website. They were patient and thoughtful in response to my requests. When they promised something by a certain date, they delivered. I especially appreciate Speakeasy's common sense approach to the marketing of professional services. They really "get it. Thanks for the good work."

— *David R. Hagen, Esq.*

****

"The Process Of Creating The Books Is Very Easy."

From a sampling of questions Speakeasy provided I was able to add and expand the information, I knew my clients needed. The staff was very easy to work with. I highly recommend the Speak A Book process to any attorney who wishes to give his potential clients a better understanding of the legal process. I give a copy of my book to every person who consults with me on their recent pending charges."

— *Ronnie M. Cole, Esq.*

****

"The Process Was Easy And I Give Speakeasy A Five."

"You walked me through every step of the process, but the book still came out how I wanted it: in MY voice. I would recommend the process to almost anyone who wants instant credibility. The book is a walking advertisement that I routinely give out to new clients. By having your book, you are showing that you are a specialist that is here to stay. Highly recommend."

— *Brad J. Balke, Esq.*

****

"Speakeasy's System Is Ideal To Get Your Book Out There In Writing Quickly And Easily"

"I highly recommend the Speakeasy company for publishing your book. First, their phone-interview, 'talk-your-book' system is ideal for those of us with writer's block to get your book out there in writing quickly and easily. Most of us can talk for hours about our fields, but when it comes time to write, we suffer from paralysis due to over-analysis. The solution is Speakeasy. Second, nothing separates you from your competitors like expertise. And nothing says expertise better than a book written by you. I couldn't recommend them highly enough."

— *Gordon Levinson, Esq.*

****

ABOUT THE AUTHOR

 Richard Jacobs is the author of:

- "But I Only Had 2 Beers!" (Truth talk from over 25 DUI lawyers)

- Secrets of Attorney Marketing Law School Dares Not Teach (1st, 2nd & 3rd Editions)

- The Attorney Authority Reboot

- The 12 Powerful Principles of Prosperous Law Practices

- The Virtual Closing System (closing potentials when you <u>CAN'T</u> get-'em-in-the-office or they won't come)

- The Ultimate Guide to Local Business Marketing by Perry Marshall (Richard Jacobs contributing author)

<u>Richard has spoken about Attorney Marketing at:</u>

- NACDL Las Vegas DUI Conference
- PILMMA (Personal Injury Lawyers Marketing & Management Association)
- DUIDLA Arizona Conference

- Perry Marshall & Associates Small Business Marketing Conference
- Local Lawyer Meetup Groups in Dallas, Long Island, NY, Milwaukee, and Los Angeles)

Richard specializes in helping attorneys break free from 70-hour work weeks and marginal law practices. Through his work at Speakeasy Marketing, Inc, he has helped over 1,000 attorneys nationwide transform their lives, bank accounts, and law practices into successful, revenue producing businesses.

Starting in 2009 with the growth of myDUIattorney.org from scratch into a nationwide advertiser for DUI attorneys, Richard works with solos and small law firms in 17 different practice areas (including Family Law, Personal Injury, Criminal Defense, Immigration and more) to learn, implement, and profit from sound marketing that law school dares not teach.

If you are ready to improve your law practice and break free of mediocrity & struggle, contact Richard Jacobs today at: (888) 225 - 8594 or visit **www.SpeakeasyMarketingInc.com**

Table of Contents

15

BROAD-BASED PRACTICE AREA(S) VS. NICHE, TARGET MARKETS

In a recent dream, I thought up a book title: "The 7.5 Billion Reasons Why You Should Target and Niche Yourself in Your Market". In the dream, I was explaining to someone why you should have a target market, why you should niche yourself down and why you can't afford to advertise to everybody. In the dream, I was talking to someone who was selling a product.

Richard: ('R') "Let's say it costs you one dollar to sell to someone your product. The whole world is your market, so you have to spend $7.5 billion to sell your product to everyone. What will happen?"

In the dream the person I was speaking with ('P') said: "I'd be out of money in two seconds. I couldn't do that."

R: "Let's say, instead, you're targeting just the United States. We are cutting out everyone else in the world, so that leaves approximately 350 million people. That's at one dollar per person. Now you only have to spend $350 million instead of $7.5 billion total. Can you do that?"

P laughed and said, "There's no way I could do that. That's crazy."

R: "Let's niche down more. What state are you in?"

P: "I'm in Texas.".

R: "That's good because now instead of 350 million people, in Texas there are only 37 million people that live there. Great. So, can you afford $37 million to market?"

P: "No, I can't. That's still way beyond my budget."

R: "That's okay. Don't worry about it. What do you do for work?"

P replied, "I'm a DWI attorney in Texas."

R: "Wonderful. So, would you say you're looking for people that are over 18 years old? And people that can drive?"

P: "Well, yes, that's who I'm looking for."

R: "If you market to someone that is five years old, would that help you? Because you know they can't get a DUI, right?"

P: "Well, no, that wouldn't help me."

R: "Well, I've got good news for you. Instead of 37 million people in the state of Texas, let's say there are only 27 million, for easy math, who are under the age of 18. That only leaves 10 million people left for you. Can you afford that?"

"I still can't afford that," P insisted.

R: "That's okay. We're getting closer. At least you don't have to spend 7.5 billion dollars. All right, so we're looking for people over 18. How about the upper limit for age? How about the lower limit for age?"

P: "It really would be better to have someone who is probably 30 to 60 years old. Outside of that, they're either just frankly too old and unlikely to get a DUI or too young to have any money for the case".

R: "I've got great news for you. Out of the 10 million people, there are only about two million people that fit that criteria. We're getting a lot closer. I forgot to ask… what city you are in?"

P: "I'm in San Antonio."

R: "Okay, great. Well, again, I've got great news for you. Out of those two million, there are only 400,000 people in San Antonio proper that fit that criteria. Where are you at in San Antonio? It's a big place."

P: "I'm on the South side."

R: "How far do you think people will go to see a lawyer?"

P: "I would say probably a half hour drive is the max."

R: "Again, I have great news for you my friend. Out of the 400,000 people we are talking about, there are roughly 80,000 that meet that criteria. Now we're getting warmer."

"But I still can't afford to market to all of those people", P complained.

R: "Now you've got to start thinking more deeply. What else about them might be in common? They have to have a valid driver's license, right? Is there a way you could figure that out? Do more men or women that get charged with DWI? Where do people tend to get DWIs?"

P: "I often hear that my clients are coming home from a bar or from a friend's house. Sometimes they're leaving a sporting event."

R: "So for this group of people, in this geographic area, approximately this age range, who tend to go to bars, clubs, sporting events & friends' houses, who are 60% men, who are more often Hispanic, is there anything you can do to target them on Facebook, Instagram, Google Pay Per Click, TikTok, Snapchat, Sports aficionado websites, concert ticket websites (with banners), through direct mail or any similar methods?"

The discussion continues, and my dream ends.

My dream represents a similar exercise that you must go through when you're looking to attract new clients.

Remember: no attorney has enough money to market to everyone – you're not McDonalds or Starbucks. Work through this niche-ing down process until you get close to your ideal customer avatar.

How to Find Your Ideal Client Avatar

Some of the parameters you should consider are: Gender, age range, hobbies, self-employed vs. wage earner, marital status, with or without kids, income level, political affiliation, religious affiliation, cultural influences (ex: Hispanics appear to be more cash and family oriented, and make decisions in groups vs. individually), language preferences (Chinese clients may prefer a Chinese-speaking attorney), sexual orientation (LGBT-friendly lawyers should say this on their websites and in their marketing to attract these types of clients)

Where do your prospective clients like to go? Do they eat out at restaurants a lot? Do they drive their kids around? Do they live in individual homes or apartments? Then consider what kind of circumstances led to the problem that they are now facing? These questions should be applied to the market and type of client you most wish to represent.

Trust me, **you have an ideal client**. Any attorney that tells me that everyone is their client is usually a mediocre earner and not very successful.

Consider how insurance companies profile their customers... Younger people are known for risky behaviors and are charged higher insurance rates; same for people who drive sports cars; it's assumed that a sports car owner will drive faster and be involved in more accidents and acquire more traffic tickets. Insurance companies set premiums for evidence-based reasons and are constantly data-mining to determine their rates. They aggressively and actively profile their clients to discern and minimize their risk and their revenue. You can and should apply the same tactics to marketing to your target clients.

Focusing Your Marketing Budget on Highly – Matched Avatar Clients

Let's say you have an ad budget of $1,000 and you have 10,000 potential prospects. This means you could spend 10 cents on each and to get in front of all of them.

Instead, what if you take the number of general prospects from 10,000 down to 5,000 juicy, targeted prospects who are more likely to have the characteristics or circumstances of good clients? In that case, you can now spend 20 cents (2x) on each prospect because these are better quality leads.

What if your competitors, because they don't know how to niche down, are only spending 10 cents on every prospect with a pulse who can fog a mirror?

Because you now know the value of niching, you spend 50 cents on 2,000 well-qualified prospects vs 10 cents on 10,000 prospects.

You're now spending five times more, on higher quality leads, yet you're spending the exact same $1,000 your competitors are. You've taken the time to niche them down and understand who they really are. Yes, you're missing out on 8,000 potential prospects, some of whom would actually make good clients, BUT...

What do you think will happen if you're spending 5x what your competitors are on the good prospects? You can send them 5x the marketing messages. You can send marketing messages more often. You can send higher quality marketing messages. Your conversion rate of initial consult to retainer-paying client will be much higher, emboldening you continue niche-ing and profiting.

Examples of Niche-ing For Several Practice Areas

The following ideas may be useful, or you may wish to focus on the opposite or a different mix. They are examples ONLY from successful lawyers I know and work with:

Criminal Defense:
- Misdemeanors only, not felonies
- Focus on sex crimes, as many attorneys find them distasteful, yet defendants pay well due to high stakes
- DUI / DWI only
- Vehicle-related crimes only

Family Law:
- High net-worth divorce
- Self-employed people (business owners with lots of assets)
- Domestic violence within a marriage dissolution, emergency removals
- Divorce with custody issues

- Forensic accounting expert on staff – master at finding hidden assets

Personal Injury

- Trucking or motorcycle accidents
- Slip & Fall
- Medical Malpractice during COVID-19
- Car accidents

Estate Planning

- Will contests
- Probate specialist
- Special Needs Trust
- Dementia / Alzheimer's-related care
- Elder Abuse
- Long-term care plans

Business Law:

- Commercial lease disputes
- New company formation
- Contractual breaches / Specific performance
- Mergers & Acquisitions

PRINCIPLE #2:

MINDING YOUR MINDSET

Before you mistakenly think: "I don't want to hear about mindset," please realize... it is super important. Have you ever been treated rudely by someone at the coffee shop, only to have it ruin your whole day, make you yell at your co-workers, be rude to clients, come home, get into a fight with your spouse, and make you feel like you're the worst person in the world?

How about navigating the 2020 Corona Virus Pandemic? You think that every single person in the entire world didn't have to deal with fear, anxiety about their health, their business, their friends, family, their nation, and the future? Without the right mindset and attention to it, without actively working on your inner game and your thought patterns, your entire life could be prosperous, or it could descend into the depths of depression quickly.

Here's something else I've discovered (Obvious? Common sense? Sure, but informative):

In every city, every county, in every state in the United States, there are attorneys (sometimes in the same office building, sometimes across town) who are experiencing success or failure in the SAME PRACTICE AREA.

Some are doing phenomenally well, grossing $500,000, even one million dollars a year. Others are barely scraping by, sitting in their offices with cobwebs on their phones, wondering how they're going to survive.

This phenomenon goes for EVERY PRACTICE AREA, EVERY CITY, EVERY CLIENT POPULATION, without exception. I have spoken to 1,000+ attorneys all over the United States, and it's revealing to hear what they say.

The lawyers I've spoken to who are failing are always ready with a list of excuses as to why it's not working for them.

- "You don't understand. People in this city have no money."
- "In this economy, no one can afford a lawyer."
- "My competitors spend $100k a month on marketing – I can't compete!"
- "It's impossible to get to the top of Google and beat out so-and-so. They're got it on lock."

How CAN I Instead of Why I Can't

Lawyers who prosper all have an abundance mindset and a positive outlook. Glass half full. They say to themselves: "How CAN I make it work, instead of: 'That won't work because x'". How Can I – opens up your mind to figuring out solutions. I Can't, or "That' Won't Work", closes off your mind to solutions and is the easy way out. It requires no thought and no effort to say. What good does it do you? Nothing.

Aspiring attorneys... no matter how successful they are, continually strive for more and better. Formulating new marketing strategies; utilizing the latest marketing tactics and platforms; systematizing their practice; working on growth and improvement.

...and the attorneys who are NOT doing well? They're in 'blame mode'. They feel victimized by their profession, by their believed lack of opportunity in their given metro and practice areas. "I've tried THAT and it didn't work," and they leave it at that. Do they magically improve? Not without changing their mindset and developing new mental tools to help themselves.

"I tried X and it didn't work for me."

Because it's not helpful to you to only lecture you about having a better mindset, let's dive deeper into the comment above:

Let's use the example of Facebook Marketing for a family law attorney. They "tried it" and it "didn't work".

What does "didn't work" mean?

Did you track your spending? Was it breakeven, or 'not profitable enough', or a minor or major loss?

Did you do the work yourself or did you hire a vendor to do it for you?

What outcome did you expect? Were you advertising to get potential clients to call, email, text, or live-chat?

How much do you charge a typical, low-end family law client? (ex: $5,000). How much are you willing to pay to get a phone call from a potential client? (ex: $1,000 or $5?)

What's your conversion rate on a qualified phone call or email? (ex: "I retain 1 out of every 4 viable potentials I talk to, so my conversion rate is 25%)

How much did you spend, and did you allocate enough budget and time to acquire "enough" calls or emails?

What were you offering the potential client who would be reading / watching your ads? (free consultation, case evaluation, discounted legal fees, flat fee, sensitivity to their situation, expertise in their very specific area of need, etc.)

What happens when a potential client clicks on your ad? Do you have a landing page set up for them to click through to? What's on that page? A written text article? A video? A call to action? Information or sales pitch? Expertise demonstrated? Credentials shown?

How was your advertising tracked? Did you track how many people saw your ad vs. clicked on it, vs. visited your landing page vs. watched your video for 5 seconds vs. 2 minutes vs. called you on the phone or emailed you?

Did you or your vendor identify and niche down your ideal avatar client?

Are you starting to see all the elements in play here?

Compare the following two ads:

"Los Angeles Family Law Attorney. 32 years experience. We fight for your parental rights and your right to half your spouse's assets. Call 888-555-1212 Today."

vs.

"Long term marriage on the rocks? Who gets custody of the kids? Will I have to give my partner 'half'? Local Los Angeles Divorce Lawyer Reveals All on a 15-Min Phone Call 888-555-1212."

There can be a myriad of reasons why a certain marketing approach does or doesn't work. Without defining your approach, your target, your budget, your ads, your landing page, tracking your results, tweaking, testing and course-correcting, you're unlikely to succeed.

Do this improperly, in haste, or putting it in the hands of a vendor blindly will leave you with "a feeling" that Facebook Marketing 'doesn't work', no results, and thousands wasted.

Will mindset fix all of this? No. But a 'how can' mentality will at least put you in the frame of mind to figure out how to successfully attract clients to your firm and get them paying you the retainer fees you deserve.

When it comes to marketing your practice, <u>it's okay if you don't know what to do</u>. Help is out there.

What I CAN tell you as well, is that no marketing method works for everybody. There are lawyers who love Yelp and others who think it's a money pit. Some love Google Pay per Click, or have great results from search engine optimization (SEO). Some people make 7x their money using direct mail, while others can't even break even. Some attorneys live the dream of a

100% referral business (fewer and fewer nowadays), while many attorneys get 5-10% referrals.

The top firms I've counselled that do really well are firing on all cylinders. They have tested, tweaked, and use multiple marketing methods. Combined, 3-5 marketing channels bring in a great deal of clients.

The good news? The average small solo or 2 or 3 lawyer firm doesn't need a lot of clients. A solo may do well with 100 cases a year, while a 3-person firm, with each partner attracting 70 clients a year, may be equally prosperous.

In certain practice areas (personal injury) you may need only 20 good clients a year.

If you have one marketing method and that brings in two cases a month (24 cases per year), is that a good thing or a bad thing? Is that "enough" for a given marketing method?

Perhaps that is all you can get out of that one marketing method. Add another marketing method, and maybe that gets you another three cases a month. Now you're up to five cases a month, which is 60 per year. Then let's see what happens when you add a third method that gets only one more case a month (+12 / yr) which puts you at 72 cases a year. Is that now enough for you?

Chip away at what you need to be successful. This is how I suggest you go about marketing your practice, whether you're barely making it, or you're doing well and want to add more.

Perhaps one of your goals is to get a higher dollar value per case. Let's say your practice is criminal defense. You are bringing in around $3,500 per case but your goal is to get an average of $4,500 per case this year.

How do we chip away at that next goal? What would it mean if you normally see 100 cases a year, and each case brought in $200 more? (100 * 200 = $20,000) You're not there yet, but you're $20,000 of the way to an extra $100,000 this year.

These things and more are what you need to consider with the right mindset of, "How CAN I grow my business, even incrementally or slowly?"

Positive mindset = growth = success.

Negativity = stagnation = eventual decline = failure.

TAKING CONTROL OF YOUR ONLINE PRESENCE & THOUGHT PROCESSES

I want to tell you about a 2,000-year-old philosophy called stoicism. One of the big tenets of stoicism is that you should strive to ONLY focus on things that are ***within your control***.

The things that are not within your direct control, all they serve to do is upset you, waste your time, waste your mental energy, and so on. This philosophy really helps me feel better when I'm stressed or when things are going wrong. I encourage readers to learn about stoicism because I believe it will help you tremendously with your mindset, and the daily slings and arrows of misfortune that affects us all.

I know that a lot of attorneys are in an environment where they're constantly in conflict; arguing; fighting for their clients; being in a mode of agitation; scheming to outwit their opponents; scheming to protect and shield their clients.

This constant stress would make anyone tense and not the most agreeable of people. This is why I highly recommend that you study stoicism. It has helped transform my mindset, calm me, and helps me deal with strife and issues – many people have told me that it acts as a 2nd Bible / Torah / Quran for them in times of trouble.

Spend some time thinking about your practice. Spend time reading this book and try taking even one of these concepts and applying it to your firm. Will the next year be a good year for your practice? Will it be a bad year? (note: this book is being published in 2020, in the middle of Corona Virus, and the George Floyd protests – more to come, I'm sure. None of it easy to deal with, mentally).

Is it going to be profitable or is it going to be a year full of frustration and layoffs and closings? That is up to you, in large part, because a lot of this is within your control. It is up to you based on your actions or non-actions.

Controlling Your Online Reviews

You can't control entirely the posting of bad reviews, BUT... you CAN control actively and continually asking your current, active and ongoing (and past clients) for an honest review.

If you choose not to ask for reviews out of fear that you might get a bad one, this increases the likelihood that a negative review will stand out. There will be nothing positive to shield it and put it in context. Therefore, asking for an honest review, could give you a chance to head off any upcoming problems.

For example, when asked for a review, a past client might say, "I appreciate you asking me, but I'm just not comfortable leaving a review because of X, Y, Z. I'm not happy about these things that happened in my case."

At least then you have a chance to say, "I didn't know that. Don't worry about a review for now Mr. Smith. Let me get this fixed for you."

If you get the issue fixed for the client, you can ask again later for a review. That person is even more likely to give you a good review than he or she would have before. You listened to the problem or issue. You fixed it. You made things better. This is a good example of what I have seen work. Again, if you don't ask for reviews, if you're afraid that you will get a bad review, you will lose out on the good ones as well. That's one way of taking control of something that you may think you can't.

Being De-Platformed and Censorship

Censorship from Google, Facebook, Twitter, AVVO, email services, merchant accounts, and many companies, large and small is absolutely rampant. These companies are not your friends and they will de-platform you, or in other words, kick you off their platform at a moment's notice. When you try to appeal, they will come up with a B.S. reason: "You violated our terms and conditions."

Good luck figuring out what you violated. They will never tell you what the reason actually was because they fear liability. They just give blanket statements with no real explanation. We have heard this has happened to several clients. I've had emails from attorneys on my list complaining and asking what they can do. Well, again, it's back to the issue of control.

What can you control about being de-platformed? What I recommend, is marketing on multiple platforms. That way, just like a four-legged stool, if one of your legs gets cut, at least you have three others to stand on. If you have a one-legged stool, or a one-legged marketing platform and that leg gets chopped off, you're dead. You're finished.

The before mentioned method is just one of the many ways to control your marketing. Another method is to realize what other marketing assets you can manage. One big one, as I have spoken about, is your website which is an area you can control pretty heavily; the design, the content, etcetera. This is one thing to definitely to focus on.

You can post whatever reviews you want. There is no one saying, "We're not going to post this review. We're just going to show the bad reviews". It's your website. As long as the reviews are compliant and real, you can put as much content up as you want. You don't really have to censor what you say. Sure, you could be de-indexed by Google. However, that has a much higher threshold than what is happening right now on Facebook, Twitter and other social media platforms.

Communicating Regularly with Happy, Past Clients

Another method of controlling your marketing, is by using an e-newsletter to send to past clients to stimulate referrals. You can put whatever you want in there. Additionally, direct mail can be used to target those same clients, as well as new potentials. For example, let's say you practice DUI criminal law. After 30 days of someone's arrest, attorneys are allowed to send out mailers. The bar associations have guidelines on direct mail, but they're very easy to follow. If you comply with those guidelines and you are sending a letter with good content, you can definitely get business that way.

How Potentials Are Treated When Contacting Your Office

When someone calls your office, how are they treated?

If you are not available, does your admin simply say, "The attorney is not in. Please call back later. Bye."

Or does he or she engage the potential client, with questions designed to get information and to make the person calling in with the problem, feel at ease.

If your admin is not practicing good phone etiquette and is simply saying that you are not in, without gathering any details or setting the stage for a positive client experience, get a new admin. I know what you may be thinking. I've heard this from a lot of attorneys, "I can't get rid of so-and-so. She has been with me for years."

Well, guess what? It could be costing you $50,000, $100,000, maybe even $200,000 a year in lost business just based on how an admin answers a phone and interacts with potential clients. Again, this is another method of control which will determine how you are perceived and the first impressions people who call your office will have about you.

A Potential's Experience While In Your Office

You also control what happens when someone comes into your office, what is said to them and how they're treated. You control whether you follow up with them or not. You control how you position yourself, what you say on the phone, the rates you charge, etcetera. You control many more things than you think.

SYSTEMIZATION SUCCESS

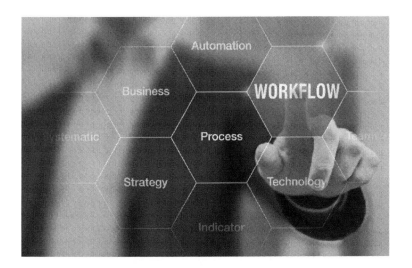

Next, we are going to talk about systematization and reducing the amount of time that you have to be chained to your law office. I did a podcast recently with a wise friend, marketer and top-notch videographer, Ron Sheetz where we discussed systematization in business.

I told Ron that, one day, I started wondering, "What does the CEO of Apple do all day?"

I realized he **can't do anything** in the business. Nothing. He has no time. He can't answer customer service calls. He can't put iPhones in a box. He can't solder a circuit board.

What he must do instead is 'steer the ship' at the highest level, using strategy, foresight and forecasting. That's his role and why he gets paid big bucks, but that's all the CEO can do. There's just no time to do anything else.

This made me realize the highest level of success I can achieve for Speakeasy Marketing, is if I wake up and I have nothing to do; the business can run completely without me.

THAT IS SUCCESS!

Even though I'll probably feel bad once I systematize Speakeasy to the point where I have nothing to do and am 100% replaceable, I will get to work on all sorts of other things with that free time. That's what I set my goal to be.

How did I (and I continue to do so) reduce my required weekly work hours at Speakeasy, yet maintain and grow its success, through systematization, procedures, and other orchestrations?

My success rests on two VITAL concepts:

- The 80/20 rule, and

- Systematization, procedures and quality checks.

I'm asked all of the time, "Rich, how do you have time to do this, that and the other?"

The answer, for the past 4 years, has been: systems, procedures and the 80/20 rule. It's been instrumental in helping me succeed in what I'm doing and also have free time to do the things I want to do. I've have been able to reduce my work week hours by 50% and it keeps improving. I fill the time with other activities, while still running a successful and GROWING business.

Do I say this to brag? Not at all. I say this to inspire and encourage YOU in your law practice. Who cares what I have done? What can you do to improve YOUR life, YOUR practice, and YOUR free time for family and other pursuits?

The amount of time that I dedicate to Speakeasy continues to reduce because it becomes more and more systematized, automated, quality-controlled and effective, without sacrificing customer service.

Your law firm and your existence outside of your professional life can also operate the same way. I don't care what practice area you're in, or what city you're in. I don't care that your clients are 'sophisticated', wealthy, poor, or simpletons. Excuses are excuses.

I know of plenty of attorneys who are able to do just what I am referring to here. One of them, a competitor of mine who appears to have a thriving and growing business is Attorney Ben Glass. Ben has nine children! He leaves the office by 5 or 6pm every day and has plenty of time to be with his family.

He is able to do this because he has systematized a lot of his business. He's an attorney in Virginia and a living example of what is possible.

These are attorneys who are willing to systematize and put procedures in place in their firm, which allows them to cut their workload.

Wouldn't that be nice? Instead of working 70 hours a week, how about 20 hours a week instead? You still can get the same amount of business, even grow, but you are now freed up to do so much more of what you want to do; whether that is focus more on your practice or other things that you may also enjoy.

Systems, procedures, and an understanding of 80/20 (the Pareto Principle) can get you there in 1 year or less.

DISPLAYING EXPERTISE THROUGH ALL POINTS OF CONTACT WITH POTENTIALS

I want to tell you about an amazing new technology that is going to be making a big-time breakout in 2020; it's called the phone. Yes, I'm being sarcastic here, but CLIO backs me up. CLIO, which does research for the legal industry, said up to 70 percent of attorneys are shopped by their potential clients by first going on Google and querying for whatever kind of attorney they need. Once they find one or two that they consider potential options, the next step is generally to call the phone number on the website.

Let's say the secretary or assistant who answers the phone says, "I'm sorry, the attorney is not here. Call back later," which is quite typical.

The person hangs up and then moves on to next listing on Google or AVVO or wherever they are searching. Let's be honest, attorneys are stacked up one on top of another in web searches, side by side, like apples at a food market.

We have done some unofficial trials to test this theory. I had my team build a list of approximately 30 or 40 attorneys and then I had my assistant call all of them. If someone answered or if someone actually got back to her, she asked them a list of questions to verify if that person is credible and usable for a particular circumstance.

Here's what happened: Out of approximately 40 professionals, approximately five of them answered. Most were not in or they didn't answer the phone. That cuts out 35 of the 40.

Of the remaining 5, we either left messages to call us back or we asked the receptionist a few questions. Again, however, the attorneys generally were never there, and we were told they would get back to us after a few days. Almost none got back to us that day.

Out of 40, we received two responses. I'm not exaggerating. Often the person answering the phone was either unqualified or simply wasn't able to help. I then went through the list again and after an average of 10 days, we would finally engage with ONE attorney who appeared to be qualified and we could hire. We had to put a ton of resources into finding someone to hire! Who is going to do that as a potential client? Not many.

Can you imagine the average person who calls and is looking for an attorney? No one is not going to call 40 different attorneys. The average potential client isn't going to have a list of prepared questions ready to vet the professional that gets on the phone. Instead, what do you think is going to happen? They're going to go with whoever answers the phone or the first to call back.

Furthermore, even for the attorney where someone does answer the phone, if that person doesn't greet the potential client the right way and doesn't provide helpful information, the caller may just hang up and move on. That's how it is nowadays. People are conditioned to price shop and they look at attorneys as interchangeable objects; that have no differentiation. As big of a problem as phone etiquette has become, it can also be a tremendous weapon.

I hear from attorneys all of the time, even our own clients:

"I answer my phone. I'm not like those other attorneys."

Sorry, but the data from HUNDREDS of calls in 7 practice areas over the years says otherwise. We call attorneys, and they're not in and many never get back to us. Attorneys unfortunately are notoriously bad at answering their phones.

Is this a big deal? Yes. Why? Because every attorney wants more clients and higher quality clients. They tell me they need more marketing. They need more leads. They need more calls. The truth is, they're really not addressing the calls and leads that they do have.

Again, CLIO's massive survey data shows 60-70% of people will shop around for an attorney. It's not just because the attorneys aren't good or that they are looking for the cheapest price. It's because no one is answering the phone or calling them back.

Why Are Lawyers So Bad At Answering Their Phones, Yet They Often Spend $15,000+ a Year on Marketing?

Why is this happening? If you're a solo practitioner, maaaaaaybe it's understandable. You can't always be there to answer the phone. You're in court, on the way to court, on the way back from court. You're dealing with clients and so on.

Totally understandable but think about getting an answering service. If and when you do, don't just have the answering service take a message so you can call the person back. Give the answering service a very simple script that will allow them to gather a few details about the potential client's case and then instruct them to say that you will return their call as soon as possible or within a day. You then get the details from the answering service and you can get back to the potential as soon as possible. The answering services should be giving you the details of that person's case and then you'll get back to them with an informed answer. If the person doesn't answer the phone, you can still leave a message saying something like, "Hi, Mr. Smith. I saw that you called earlier today about X, Y, Z. I just want to let you know, I've done a little bit of research into some of the facts of your case. I don't know them all, but I have some updated information for you that I think is timely and important. You may call me back at your convenience. My number is such and such."

This will inspire curiosity in the person that is potentially a client for you. You don't tell them exactly what you researched but by definition of being a lawyer, you will have at least thought about their case and will have a few thoughts about it to share. When they call back, that statement is true, and you can give them specifics. They will know that you cared, you listened, and you thought about them just a bit.

They are much more likely to call you back because of this curiosity factor, this personalization and because you mentioned details about their specific case. You can even get even more specific. Let's say the potential client gave a particular detail about his or her case such as they were injured when someone rear-ended their car and the at-fault party doesn't have insurance. In your message, you could say, "Hi Mr. Smith. I got your message about your rear-end collision, where you said the other person doesn't have insurance. I have some thoughts for you and some important information that is timely and important. Give me a call back. I'd be glad to discuss this all with you."

Now the potential client is going to be thinking, "Wow! This guy listened to me. He has specifics about my situation."

Guess what? You have a much higher likelihood of being called back versus just leaving a bland message or by having the person answering your phone just take a message and say you will call back.

Again, even if you're a solo attorney and you have no admin, no one to help you, you certainly can still hire an answering service to fulfill this part of your business. This will make you look a million times better than your competition and it will capture a lot of lost business that could be lost by missed calls.

If you do have admin or someone else to answer your phone, you have no excuse not to do something similar. Whoever is answering the phone can again, be given a script that will inspire the caller to have confidence in your firm and also will allow them to capture the potential's case details. You can even let your staff know that all calls coming into the office will be recorded to make sure that they are using the script effectively. There's nothing wrong with that. You have to be on top of these things. If they don't follow the scripts, again, you have to take disciplinary action. Why? Because they're letting hundreds and thousands of dollars' worth of potential revenue out the door. You have to train your admin or whoever is answering the phone to gather important details from the caller, screen for good potential clients and to make a good impression on the potential client.

Now I have dealt with thousands of attorneys over the years. Some will say they get 20-30 leads and, "None of those calls are from valid people. They were all referrals or they were all court personnel."

I can tell you this simply isn't true, but you will never know if you don't answer the phone. We actually can verify all of this by using tracking numbers. We look at the pages the potentials visited on the website before they called.

The good attorneys may only get 10-12 calls a month but they know details about every single one of those people who called because they track them all. They answer the phone. They know the deal and they can give a real honest assessment of whether those leads were good or not. Those attorneys tend to do far better and their marketing dollars go a lot further than the attorneys who are wasteful and don't answer the phone and don't bother to help themselves.

I can tell you that this is super important in this day and age of automated email responses, texting, shopping around and services like AVVO and Google and Yelp.

Remember, potential clients line up attorneys side-by-side as if they're identical widgets in a store.

Answer the Damn Phone

Answering the phone is critical. It's your chance to speak to the potential, to give them a feeling of your personality and how you work. It's a chance to defend against the chance of them just running away and hiring someone else just because the other guy answered his phone. When you answer the phone, you get a chance to evaluate whether someone is really just a tire kicker or is actually a viable client. Answering the phone is a way for you to make a connection so that you can follow up even if he or she doesn't hire you right away.

Answering the phone is a superpower - especially in this computerized AI and de-personalized world of automated interaction in 2020.

Answer the phone… and prosper.

PRINCIPLE #6:

FOLLOW-UP FAUX PAS

A quote I have attributed to myself is, "If we didn't follow-up as much as we could, and as much as we should, and as much as we do, we would have starved to death a long time ago."

As you can see from my picture, I'm not exactly "starving to death", as one wise marketing coach once told me in a tongue-in-cheek way. My company provides marketing services to attorneys. We have to work on them often times for months, sometimes years to get attorneys on as clients. We know, attorneys are busy people. They are smart people. They are well-educated people. However, it takes a bit of pursuit to sign them on. If we didn't do that, Speakeasy Marketing would be a shadow of itself. We would have been out of business a long time ago.

I hear comments like, "Rich, I love your emails. I've been following you for a year now. We just lost our SEO provider and I wanted to talk to you about helping us."

Another comment I hear often is, "Rich, I've been reading your emails for several months now and I think I'm ready to pull the trigger. Contact me."

Or, "Rich, I've been reading your emails for years and I really appreciate what you've had to say. I do have a question about this one situation. Can you help?"

I've also had emails saying, "Rich, stop pestering me. Your emails are driving me crazy. Take me off your list."

Generally, the number of good outweighs the number of bad. The truth is, however, I wouldn't have gotten any of it if I didn't follow up. With your potential clients, if you think following up is bothering them, it's unethical, if they really wanted you, they would just jump on you and hire you, that is out-of-date thinking. This mentality is not going to serve you well in this modern world.

Let me tell you about your customer, if you don't already know. They are very distracted. They're on their phones all the time. They're getting notifications from Facebook and Twitter, receiving texts and phone calls. Their mind is fragmented because they are conditioned to being pulled by all of this technology.

If I'm sitting there and I have a phone laying on the table next to me turned face up, I can't help but look at it. I've been in my email account and I've said to myself, "Stop it! Stop it! Stop it!".

The allure of notifications and the fear of missing out can be irresistible. Have you ever sat at a restaurant or a bar where there's a TV on and you're there with someone and you can't help but watch it? Or God forbid you have a phone at a lunch meeting and the person says, "Just hold on a second, one second," and they keep looking at their phone and they go, "Oh what were we talking about?".

This is happening to your potential customer while they are searching for an attorney to help them with whatever their situation may be. It's also happening to them at a time where something bad may be going on in their life. They are going to be distracted. Their mind is not focused, and they may even be afraid and upset with whatever is happening.

Your potential clients have a lot going on in their minds when they are seeking out an attorney's service. Think about it. With regard to family law, maybe it's someone who has just been served divorce papers or perhaps the potential is fighting with their ex over custody. When it comes to estate planning it could be that a loved one has died or is dying. If it's a criminal defense attorney that is being sought out, it probably goes without saying, this is a tumultuous time in this person's life.

That's the unfortunate position you're in as an attorney. It's your job to help these people. However, these people are incredibly distracted and busy. On top of that, and as I spoke about earlier, often potential clients assume all attorneys are the same. They are lined up side by side, in web searches like cartons of milk in a store. The customer is thinking, "Everyone's educated and a lot of them have been an attorney for

20 years. Everyone seems aggressive. Everyone seems like they will fight for me."

Unfortunately, this is the environment that your clients are swimming in which is why follow-up and making a good impression is so important.

Now I'm going to add on one more layer of problems. As I talked about earlier, most attorneys don't answer the phone. If their admins are answering the phone, a lot of them are turning off potential clients. The most common answer to a phone call I have found is, "Law office of Attorney Smith. I'm sorry. He is not here. He is in court today. Please call back later."

Well, if that is the case, that is going to be the end of that lead. They will move on and call the next attorney they see in Google, Yelp or AVVO.

Let's say you do get on the phone with a potential client, you've talked to them about the facts of their case and this person seems somewhat viable. Now they say, "I need to think about it." Or, "I have to wait until my wife or husband gets home. I'll get back to you."

Is that potential client coming back? Maybe. Hopefully. However, often they won't because external distractions will set in. Family members may be saying, "Why are you talking to that person? Your uncle can handle this. He's a lawyer and lawyers all do the same stuff."

Or the potential is getting back online and finding the next attorney on Google, Yelp, etcetera. This is what happens to your client after they get off the phone with you. Even if you have given them a fantastic information and filled them with hope for the future, chances are, distraction, time, fear and uncertainty will creep in. All of this will conspire against this potential hiring you. They're not going to remember who they spoke to. They're just going to go back to Google and find the next guy. Or perhaps someone else will have followed up with them and they might even attribute your meaningful initial phone call, to this other attorney. They may not even remember your name. All the work you did to pitch them could be used for them to hire some other attorney. This is why follow up is crucial.

Sure, you may annoy a few people. You will probably have some people say, "Oh, I already hired someone. Thanks, bye."

Others will hang up on you. There will be people who will say, "Don't call me. Why are you calling me?"

There will be all variations of negative responses, but guess what? You are also going to get good responses. You will get more business. You will get more clients. What would you rather have? Some of the bad, but a lot of good? Or nothing at all?

Follow-up is the key. Now, you also need to decide, how much is too much follow-up? How much is not enough? I recommend at a minimum, you follow-up with any potential client three times after the first call or email.

Now, if that person is on a really short timeline such as if they are facing DUI charges, it's probably okay to follow-up just about every day. If the prospect is on a longer timeline, let's say it's a divorce he or she is facing, I would still do the first follow up. However, I would then maybe wait two days after the initial call, then another four, then seven, etcetera. That would probably be a good starting framework for your follow-up.

Now, what does follow-up look like? The follow up can come from you in terms of a phone call, a text, email, or even direct mail.

A mixture of all of these things would probably be best. Do you, personally, have to do the follow up? Not necessarily. You can have your admin call and mention one or two particulars from the case. He or she can call and say, "Hi. This is so-and-so from the Law office of John Smith. I don't know the facts of your case. I'm not allowed to, but John did say there is one urgent issue pertaining to your driver's license that he has some updated information on. So, if you want to give us a call back, we will be glad to talk to you about that."

Whatever it may be, a well-crafted message inspires curiosity. It's not a lie because chances are, by the time they call back, you will have looked at their case, even for a minute or two. It's a very good way to get those potentials back, to show them that you've listened to what happened and that you care. This follow up is incredibly important. When doing each of the follow up attempts, I would add slightly different information.

If a deadline is approaching, let's say contesting the loss of a driver's license or going to the doctor after an auto accident, include the urgency in your follow-up communications. You might say, "I just want you to know there's a deadline coming up regarding your case. It doesn't have to be with me, but if you don't resolve this, that deadline will pass, and it will impair your ability to get the results you want in your case."

There is nothing wrong with saying that and creating urgency. Try it. Commit to at least three follow-ups. Test it. Tweak it and see what works. Review the kind of responses you're getting. You will get more business out of the same money you're spending; the same lead pool you already have.

This will help grow your business. It will give you the resources to do even more marketing and to expand your practice.

FINDING THE JUICY LOPSIDEDNESS OF YOUR PRACTICE AND CAPITALIZING ON IT

I want to talk about interesting things that you can learn by looking at your past clients. If I asked you what makes a good client, I'm sure you could tell me. I've convinced a few attorneys to look through their past client files and tell me what similarities they see.

I ask them, "Do you notice a certain age range that made for better or worse clients? Were there more men or more women clients? What were the ethnicities? What were the circumstances of their case and which cases did you win? Who were the judges? Who were the prosecutors?".

You may think you have this idea in your mind of what your client base has been; who was a good client and who was bad. However, when I did this experiment, a lot of the attorneys found out there were a lot of skews; things they didn't realize that were there lying in their old client base.

So, what do we do with this information? We used this to help change who they were targeting as potential clients. One of the attorneys we work with discovered that in Northern California, specifically Napa County, the cases were handled a lot different than in other courthouses in the area. Another attorney we asked found that there were two insurance companies that he had worked with on personal injury cases, where the settlements on average were much larger than results in other cases he had won. By taking the time to go back and review past client files, these skews were found, which can be particularly helpful when it comes to targeting your market.

When you change and improve your targeting, you're better able to avoid people that wouldn't make good clients. You will then be able to avoid wasting your marketing dollars on those people and redirect resources toward viable clients.

I'm going to expand upon this a little bit now. Look at the number of calls that came into your office and who took the calls. Look and see the kind of cases that you were able to land and the dollar amounts. What were the particulars in your cases versus those that your law partner took? Let's say you're Caucasian and your law partner is Hispanic. You may notice, for some reason, that your Hispanic law partner lands more Hispanic clients. Now he probably didn't target Hispanic clients, but perhaps when the clients initially called in, they felt an affinity toward him because he has a Hispanic last name, or he is bilingual. What about the conversion rate when you answer the phone versus when your admin answers the phone? Maybe you land the client 55% of the time, but when your admin answers the initial call and you do the follow up, you are only converting 20% of the time. This might tell you there might be a problem with your admin answering the phone. Something is going wrong here, and you are losing potential clients.

Let's say you work with a few other attorneys in your practice. Your conversion ratio on landing clients is a 33% but one of the other attorneys is closing 61% of the potentials that come across her desk. What is she doing different? Talk to her. Ask her about her calls and see what's going on. There are always skews there's always lopsidedness in business. I see it everywhere. I expect it. If you do the same, you will find it. You can use these skews and capitalize on them to improve your business; it's like alchemy. You don't necessarily have to invest more money in marketing. Instead you can start with internal tweaks that will help get you more money and more juice out of your business. This is a thinking exercise. Yes, it takes time but use any downtime you may have. What better way to spend it than to think about things like this and make the next year a fantastic year for your business.

SUCCESS RARELY HAPPENS ON THE FIRST, EVEN FIFTH ATTEMPT

I want to talk about the magic of the number 100; One hundred attempts at doing something. I've been through the process of getting to this number many times. It really is magical and I'm going to explain a couple of reasons why. Here at Speakeasy Marketing, when we create a new attorney's website from scratch, we redesign it and we change what was there before. We have this big checklist to ensure we are addressing every possible component of creating a new site. Currently this list has

74 items on it. However, we have revised this checklist literally a hundred times.

Is that good or is that bad? The fantastic thing is, that because we have done all of these tweaks and changes to the list, it has become so robust, that we can now redesign a client's website and get it live much quicker than we did before; probably in about 10 days if we really push. It used to be 30-40 days. I don't have to do much. Once we set the process in motion, my team knows how to do it. What I noticed is that it took about 100 attempts or 100 revisions to get this list just right.

I have noticed this in other arenas as well. For example, I do a number of podcasts on various topics. I do one on attorney marketing. I have another on the topic of future technologies. I've had one focused on the Bitcoin realm, etcetera. What I've noticed, is when I first do my first few interviews on any given topic, it can be kind of awkward. I am not yet familiar with the lingo in that industry. I don't know the players. So, I start out asking basic questions. As I keep doing the interviews, I naturally start to learn more and become more comfortable with the given topic. I have noticed that by about the tenth interview, I'm starting to become conversant with the language of that industry. My questions are getting better and after I have done about 30, I then start discovering who the real experts in the industry are. I keep going and going and by the time I've done 100 podcasts in a given industry, I know a lot of people. I know who knows who and I can make connections with people. I've almost become an insider in that industry. I know the lingo. I know a lot of the concepts. I actually can come up with new ideas to help improve that industry. I get almost a 10,000-foot view of what's going on.

How does this apply to your law practice? When you get clients in a particular practice area, you may not have thought to look back on them and to look for correlations, but they're there. Let's use the example of a personal injury attorney. After hundreds of accident cases, you know which insurance companies pay out and which ones fight you to the death. You know if your client was cited at the scene, if their case is doomed or if they still have a good chance for recovery.

If you want to grow your practice, you can't just do things once and say, "Oh, it didn't work."

You can't just work on your phone scripts at your office and make one tweak and say, "Oh, it didn't work."

You can't just try Yelp or ask a client for a review and they don't give you one and you say, "Oh, it didn't work. I give up."

If you try 100 attempts at anything, chances are you are going to get really good at it. If you want to know why that other attorney has so many reviews on Google Maps and you don't have any, maybe it's because you haven't tried enough times. Now you may not need to try exactly 100 times to get the results, but anything you put that much effort into, even if it's small, over and over, you are going to get pretty good at it.

I want you to be observant as you go through your 100 attempts at whatever you need to do. Observant meaning do not give up at one. Don't give up at five. Don't give up at 10. Start paying attention to what you are learning from each try. After maybe 60-70 attempts, you may be thinking you are really making some headway. Then at 100 attempts, you might decide you have the system or the tactic down pat. At that point, you should still sit back and say to yourself, "Are there any other refinements to make this better?"

It's worth it to improve your business and to improve your life. I hope this helps you with your practice. Look at it. Think about it. Apply it and watch the magic come from it.

WHICH MARKETING PLATFORMS ARE BEST AND HOW MANY SHOULD YOU ADVERTISE ON?

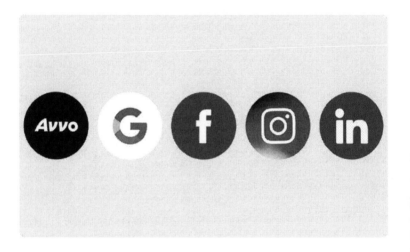

You may have noticed I haven't yet talked about specific marketing platforms. Why do you think that is? As I've alluded to before, there is no one marketing platform that works for everybody. You have to try a number of marketing platforms and have several running simultaneously, in order to have a solid practice. The trouble is that you won't know which ones are the right ones right off the bat. You have to experiment. You certainly can't throw in the towel having tried any of them just once, as I alluded to in the last chapter.

In this chapter we will now talk about various marketing platforms and what to do to get better at them. You don't want your 100 attempts at a marketing effort, to just be blind arrows shot at a target. How do you narrow it down and get good at a particular marketing channel?

Let's start with AVVO. Start by looking at other attorneys in your practice area. Note who is coming up first. Who is paying for advertising? When they rank really well, what appears to be the factors that are getting them there? Is it the number of reviews they may have? Are there keywords in their reviews? For example, let's say you're a DUI lawyer in Atlanta, Georgia. Do a lot of the reviews have the words DUI attorney, DUI lawyer or drunk driving lawyer, Atlanta and Georgia in them?

That may be a factor. Do the top-ranking attorneys have only reviews listed that high-ranking, with few or low-ranking reviews? Do they have a lot of accolades from peers and not just from clients? Do they have aspects of their profile that are fully filled out and yours is blank or limited? Are there other factors that are appearing to modulate what's going on with their profile?

Whatever platform you're on, you should also pay attention to the ads. Who is advertising? What keywords are they using? What are they saying? What calls to action do they have? Let's say you're on Yelp, the same things should be applied. How many reviews, what do the reviews say, what's the placement? And on and on.

You may not want to do this. You may think, "I'm not going to sit there and analyze this stuff. My SEO guy is supposed to do that."

While that may be true, they might not do it without some prompting. A nice thing to do would be to have a checklist to apply to any given marketing platform you are using to find out if you're really maxing out your opportunities; to see if you can improve your performance. There are going to be a lot of elements that are common to every platform, such as reviews. However, there are also many other factors that you will note are the same or similar on all platforms as well.

You should also have your SEO company look at the platforms you use and note what is not there. This is harder, but it is a really important part of the analysis. If something jumps out at you, then maybe you should incorporate that one thing into your profile or website, or whatever it is you are using. Don't just think, "It's not there because it doesn't work."

People may not be doing it but that could be for many different reasons. For example, a family law attorney might list 10 different types of cases they handle under this practice area and you only generally take on divorces, emergency removals and child custody disputes.

Let's say you do not handle annulments. Maybe you should include all of that in your profile; what you don't do and what you do. Maybe no one else is differentiating themselves that way. They're just saying, "I do family law," or, "I do personal injury cases."

Maybe they're not specifying that really, they only take on cases dealing with trucking accidents or they only take on cases with serious injury. There are many permutations here that you can consider. What's seen and what's unseen will help you and work for you on any platform; even with direct mail.

I work with attorney clients that are doing direct mail, so I asked, "Do you get letters?"

"No. But our clients get letters from other attorneys. Sometimes they bring them in," the answer often is.

I say, "Ask your clients as much as possible about those letters, whether they hire you or not. Photocopy them if it's okay with the prospective client so you can study what is in each one."

That's another great way to analyze what the competition is doing. Get your hands on any direct mail pieces that other attorneys may be doing and see what they are doing. Maybe there are things that's going out there, that are not online. Maybe they are savvier or have different things to say. If you look at all the marketing platforms in a given practice area, or you have your admin do this for you, look at what's being done across all of these platforms. Maybe some of the platforms have really compelling items while other platforms don't. Just because someone should take what works well in a Google pay-per-click ad and replicate that on their website, they may not be doing it. They may not have that thinking. This is yet another permutation of how you can improve your marketing; regardless of the platform.

HOW TO DISPLAY AUTHORITY, EXPERTISE, AND CREATE DESIRABILITY TO HIRE YOU

Why Author a Book to Build Your Law Practice?

Authoring a book on your practice area gives the perception that you're not just another attorney who has "20 years of experience, is aggressive and will fight for you." While you are all of those things, you also become an author of a book, which gives you authority in that practice area.

Nowadays prospective clients can just scroll through lists of attorneys they find online. If you look at AVVO, Yelp or any of these platforms, there are dozens of attorneys that all look the same at first glance. These platforms are set up with templates that make you look exactly the same as all the other attorneys listed there. Therefore, you have to do the extra work to make yourself stand out.

Unfortunately, we often find that the things attorneys think would make them an authority in their practice area to a prospective client, really aren't doing much at all. For example, "20 years' experience", unfortunately doesn't mean much. A lot of attorneys can say this. The same could be said about noting you are "board certified"; it doesn't mean much to a potential client. Using lines like, "We are aggressive!", "I will fight for you!", or "We offer free consultations," doesn't set you apart from the competition anymore.

The question then becomes, what can you do to really make yourself stand out? This has been a big part of Speakeasy Marketing's success. I authored "Secrets of Attorney Marketing Law School Dares Not Teach." It's now in its third edition and is listed on Amazon, Kindle and Audible. I put my accumulated knowledge into a book, and it has brought me tons of business. It has truly been instrumental in growing this company. It has kept me in the game for 10 years of working with attorneys and helping them grow their businesses. Once I saw the book was tremendously successful for me, I realized I needed to be doing this for my clients to get them more cases and better cases.

I can tell you that I have heard directly from hundreds of my clients who say, "Hey, Rich, I got your book. I love it. I learned a lot from it. I've read it cover to cover. Now what can you do for me?"

That sort of statement is very telling. When I started hearing that, I thought, "Wait a minute. You just said you read the book cover to cover. Now you're asking me what I can do for you? That doesn't make any sense."

I realized you can tell someone all about what you do, but it doesn't mean they want to go ahead and actually do it themselves. However, this was a great conversation opener. This was building me as an attorney marketing authority above and beyond every other SEO company out there. Having a book has been instrumental to my business.

This notion of creating authority in this field has been responsible for probably 70 to 80% of my success with Speakeasy Marketing. I encourage you to at least take a look at this and consider it. It's something you really need to do to stand out from your competition. There are still only very few attorneys in many metro areas and in many practice areas that have written books. That means there is plenty of room for you to become the authority.

We've been doing the Speak-a-Book process for eight years now, and in total, created over 300 books for our attorney authors. The whole point of doing something like this, is to raise your stature as an attorney; to separate you from the pack.

I recently did an interview with Tracy Merda of Speakeasy Publishing, our attorney authority publishing imprint where we create Speak-a-Books™. The process for creating these books includes conducting a 90-minute, recorded interview with an attorney in order to create the content.

We then transcribe, edit, re-format and hone the interview transcript and make it into a book written by that attorney.

The wonderful immediate benefit is that this doesn't take a lot of effort on the part of the attorney to do this. The heavy lifting and most of the work is done by Speakeasy, not the attorney. The goal of this process is to create a finished book in 30 days from start to finish, not 7-10 years (the typical amount of time it takes without this process).

I have included the interview Tracy and I did together, where we go in depth on how and why this process works. There are at least 10 reasons why authoring a book will help you. I encourage you to at least read the following interview and come to your own conclusions...

THE 80/20 RULE

I use a principle in my life and in my business extensively. It's called the 80/20 principle, or the Pareto principle. I also call it the skew or the lopsidedness. It's a way to supercharge everything you do. It's a way to spend a lot less time getting done whatever it is you're working on. It's a way to focus on the most important minority or small part of what you do that has the greatest effect on what you do.

It's a way to completely revolutionize your practice. It will help you get more done in a quarter of the time that it takes most people to do it. This is no exaggeration. I've noticed everywhere in life and in business, there's a lopsidedness; there's the skew to everything. I'm going to give you an example.

I've looked at well over 1000 attorney websites over the past 10 years. Approximately 80% to 90% of the traffic to those websites, without fail goes to only five or six pages. If you want to improve the traffic to your site, which pages should you work on? Should you work on all of the pages? Or, should you work on these top five or six pages? Those pages represent the lion's share of your traffic and if the lion's share of your traffic enters in through those few doors, guess which entry points should look the best and help you get the most business?

What if those highly visited pages on your site cover practice areas you don't want to focus on, or the pages just seem to be worthless to you? You could either change the content on those pages or build up other pages that are close to the top that also get a decent amount of traffic. That's just a quick example of a few things we do for our attorney clients and that you can do for yourself. You can go to Google Analytics and sort it by the number of people visiting a page. I would sort it over the past three months, six months or even a year. You will very quickly see your top pages.

Some of the pages with the highest amount of traffic are obvious, such as your home page. Others may not be so obvious, such as an article you wrote that for some reason is getting a lot of traffic. Some of them may reveal things to you that aren't helpful. An example might be if you are a criminal defense attorney and you wrote an article on Miranda rights that is getting a lot of traffic. Sure, you may get the visits to that page, but it might not be bringing in any actual business. What you can do, is fix that page by adding relevant content that will bring in cases. That is one example of the 80/20 rule.

Let's look at the cases that you do. I guarantee you that even though the fact patterns are different in every case, there are probably anywhere from two to five major flavors of case that you handle. For instance, if you practice DUI defense, there are going to be cases that are very similar. A lot of your clients may have failed the breath test or refused the breath test. Maybe there is a whole slew of people that failed the field sobriety tests and so on. The point is, you can identify the majority of your cases have certain common characteristics. What documents, for instance, come up in those scenarios? What's the timeline of those scenarios? What's the average amount of money you need to charge to be profitable in those scenarios?

When potential clients call, you can let them know this case is very similar to what cases you typically handle. You can let them know right away what's going to happen, what your responsibilities are to them, the documents they may need to fill out, etcetera. That will command and communicate confidence and it will get the case done faster. Once you've identified all of this, now what do you do?

Let's say you generally handle four different types of cases. Look amongst those four types. I would bet the documents involved are pretty similar across the board. Why not have templates for all of those documents, where you only have to fill in a few things in order to personalize the forms and make them complete. You can train your admin to do all of this. This will help you streamline your practice to become a lot more efficient and you can cut out wasted time on repetitive tasks.

You can share this with other people in your office or it could even be automated perhaps by email or with some other kind of computerization. This whole process can be given to someone else to do the work for you entirely, so all you have to do is the top-end supervision. It doesn't matter your practice area. It doesn't matter where you work; whether it's rural or urban; none of that matters. When you look back at your past cases, you will see how all of this can be implemented and you should capitalize on that. Those are two areas where the 80/20 exists.

A third area where you can apply the 80/20 rule is going to be in your marketing. When you track your marketing, you may want to look at what is getting you the most customers, who pays their retainers and what are the most profitable cases.

You can react to that in different ways. You can cut out the things that are not working well. You could also look and say, if method A, which is my best method, gets me six cases a month and everything else gets me one or two cases, should I cut those other methods out? Or should I keep those in knowing that they are still getting me one or two cases a month. It's not a lot but it's profitable and it adds stability. May I can work on method A and make it even better. For example, let's say I'm getting a lot of business from Yelp. What can I do to make my Yelp profile even stronger? Can I get more reviews? Can I pay for a better placement? Again, if you identify the 80/20 you can capitalize on it.

The 80/20 rule exists everywhere. I derive great comfort, success and money from knowing it's always there. If you know it's always there, you just have to go find it. I'll give you another example. If you have more than two or three people answering your phone, guess what? One of those people, for some reason, is going to get the most people signing up to become clients. One of those people, for some reason, is going to get by far the least number of people signing up to be clients. What can you do with this information?

Find out what the top person is doing to get clients to convert and do the same with the person who is doing the worst. I guarantee you it's there. It's there in my business. I can tell you right now, one sales guy and one appointment center are five times better than the others I have. I'm always looking to see what this guy is doing. How can we replicate it with everyone? I have a metric now and a standard. What are the other ones doing or not doing? If one person is really falling below the standard, I know we either need to train them better or they have to be let go. I know what's possible because I see this 80/20 and this skew. Again, in your practice, look for these 80/20 opportunities and see how you can systematize even part of it.

You need to be thinking that if this element represents even somewhat of a majority in a given area, how can you work on it and begin to systematize it. Can you systematize part of it? Can you delegate part of it? Can you delegate all of it? Can you find the commonalities and make it more efficient, so it takes you half the time or a third of the time to do? This thinking is super critical. It will help your practice vastly grow. It's helped my business. We apply it to clients when they will let us. A lot are very resistant to the idea of the 80/20 rule. However, I can tell you, it's powerful when it is done right. It's made me a lot of money and has helped build my business to where it is today.

USING A BLACKOUT CALENDAR TO FREE YOUR TIME FOR SUCCESS

It happens every year. We all come back from the holiday and get caught up in January. Pretty soon, before you know it, it will be February and then all of a sudden, it's March. On we go and before you know it, you got caught up in the year's activities and there you are at the end and your results are the same as the previous year. You will just be reacting to what's going on.

If you're reading this book, it means you're ambitious. You don't want to be a run of the mill attorney and react to everything. It means you want to have a plan. I know as attorneys, you are planners. You are not just spur of the moment, fly by the seat of your pants people. Otherwise, it's unlikely that you'd be an attorney. It's rare that those personality traits coincide. Being planners, the thing I suggest you do is plan out a calendar for the coming year. If there are marketing initiatives that you want to put in, add them to the calendar. If there are certain dates that you know you're going to be gone on vacation or in court, the judges are not in or you're going to be tied up with a big case for several months and so on, put it all on your schedule now.

One thing I suggest you carve out time for, is maybe a half hour during your work time, each week or whatever you can do, where you will work on your business, on the systems, on the 80/20 and all of the things I have shared with you in this book. I want you to black it out. I want it to be an appointment that you have with yourself that cannot be cancelled. It's just as important as picking up your kid from kindergarten. No one else can pick them up. Only you can do it. You have to be at the school at this time for instance. You can't break this appointment.

If you have 52 of these sessions over the year, that's 52 times where you dedicated your time and your thoughts solely to your business; to improve it. Let's say worst case you only improve your business 1% a week. If you do that 52 times over the year, your business should be 52% better. This is what it takes. You have to do it now. If you wait until the next year comes, it's going to be a lot less effective. I highly encourage you set this time with yourself to work on your business. Thirty minutes is nothing. It will fly by.

I do this for myself, with my businesses. It is one of the most critical things I do; spending that thinking time away from distractions. Put your phone away. Close your laptop. Tell your staff you can't have any distractions, unless it is an emergency. Sit with a pad of paper, relax and think.

At the risk of telling you too much, I'm going to go a little further. I'm going to go back to this planning idea. If you plan out your year on this calendar and have it up in your office, you can look at it and it will give you context. You can view it anytime and see where you are at for the year. If you had a certain goal by end of June 1, for example, to set up two new marketing systems you will at least know where you're at with that plan. You aren't working off of a generic feeling that things are not going well or that things are probably going ok. I encourage you to stick to it. This small thing will give you a sense of place and achievement. You won't just be floating in the netherworld. You will also be less likely to make hasty decisions. For example, if a new marketing idea or a new marketing company comes to you, instead of just saying, "Yes! I need help!", you can sit and thinking about whether or not this fits within your plan.

If you don't do this, other people will make plans for you or you will be tempted to make impulse decisions. That's not how you get to your goal.

What result do you want to have this year? Do you want to have your practice stay the same? That's fine. Maybe you're in a declining market and just staying the same is good. Maybe you want it to grow by 10%, 20% or 30%. Maybe, for you, growth of 100% is unreasonable. Regardless, you have to set goals. You have to set expectations for your business.

Once you do, you can drill down and be more specific. Let's say you're a husband and wife team. The husband practices criminal defense; the wife practices family law. You sit down with your wife and you say, "Family law cases are making us $4000 in retainers. My criminal cases on average probably bring in $2000 per case. For this year, let's get some more family law cases in."

Now you have at least the outline of a plan for the year. Now that you've decided that, determine how many more family cases you want? Let's say you and your wife determine that two additional family law cases per month is reasonable.

Next, you have to figure how will you bring those additional cases in. What does our marketing look like? Where's the 80/20 in your marketing, or your personnel, your follow up, etcetera. Now, you can start working backwards and you make a plan to hit that goal. I know this is very basic information. However, you might be surprised that most people just don't do it. They claim they have no time to do it and so they just never go anywhere. Years pass by and nothing substantial happens. This is why I want you to black out these dates with yourself. If you can only spend 15 minutes focusing on your marketing and business growth, then at least do that. There's no one on earth, I don't care who you are, who can't do 15 minutes a week.

It will be a fantastic thing for you to have in motion for this year. You will be ahead of most of your competitors if you implement all of this. This will really make this next year a huge success for you.

I've given you my very best advice here. I don't ask for anything in return. You may notice in this book, there was no specific marketing platform that I talked about. There were no secret Ninja tricks on how to be better in AVVO or Yelp. I think that speaks to my experience and what I've seen that actually helps attorneys. I've given you the principles, the techniques and tactics that I honestly believe will help you. If you go through these pages and you implement the tactics and suggestions, I have given you, I guarantee your business will grow. I think after 10 years of doing this, I know what I'm doing.

I don't want anyone to be struggling or failing in their business. You spent a lot of time and effort to get where you are today. I want everyone to be prosperous and happy and have a successful practice. I encourage you to go through these pages, several times, pick the suggestions that you think are most within your reach and implement them this year.

Bonus Principle #13:

The Six Thinking Hats

Your competitors might rattle you at bit. Maybe they take cases that should be going to you, and cause you to lay awake at night worrying. You can allow them to get the best of you, or, you can do something to improve your practice, revenue and mindset. Instead of being run out of business by your competitors, there are ways to profit from them.

The first thing you can do to utilize your competitors, is to realize they are out there and want to make money just like you. They are not evil. They aren't trying to destroy you. They are just simply trying to live, make money and profit like you are. If you have that mindset, it becomes less personal.

Maybe you have the attitude that, "Oh that guy over there is my competitor. He gets all of the cases and he doesn't deserve them. I've been an attorney twice as long as he has. He knows nothing."

That kind of thinking isn't going to get you anywhere. It's just going to upset you and take up your mindshare. You will get angry, frustrated, fearful and emotional. These kinds of thoughts keep you from thinking logically. As an attorney, you must preserve your ability to problem solve. You need to be able to think rationally or you are not going to perform well in court, in your business or anywhere, for that matter.

The first thing you need to do is look internally at your emotions. Be honest and ask yourself if these competitors are getting to you. Are they getting under your skin? Are they clouding your judgement? Can you do a little bit of self-talk to turn this into logic instead?

There is a great book I recently read to my son. It's called "Six Thinking Hats", by Edward de Bono. The book discuses good decision-making techniques as six hats. Each "Thinking Hat" is a different style of thinking. For example, the White Hat is that of logic. If you have a discussion with yourself or others, you put on this hat and say to yourself, "I'm just going to think logically about this."

You then can give yourself permission two minutes later to put on the Red Hat and say, "I'm going think with emotion. How do I feel about this? Do I like this? Do I not? Am I afraid? Am I greedy? How am I feeling?"

Then, there is the Yellow Hat, which is creativity and positivity. You may ask yourself, "What is good about this situation? What is good that my competitor is doing that I am not?"

And so, on and so forth with the other hats, or ways of thinking.

Once you work on your emotions and at least, silo them, you can say to yourself, "My competitors are doing well for a reason. What is that reason?"

Then perhaps maybe you review their website and look at what they are doing for their marketing. Are they doing a newsletter? Are there any clients or potential clients that you lost to your competitor? If so, what did they say to them? What did they promise?

Instead of bemoaning, you should ask yourself, "What can I learn from all of this? What can I do to change it?"

Maybe that attorney has a great intake process and he is asking really good screening questions. Perhaps he wrote a book on the practice area I work in. Maybe that is something you should consider doing. Again, that is positive Yellow Hat thinking. Take from the negative and turn it into something you can use. I try to make this a practice in my own life. Even if I hate something, I try and look for something that I can learn from it. You know what? Ninety-nine percent of the time, I learn something. That is what it's all about. It's about improving your life and your business and not letting those negative things drag you down.

Next, we turn to the Black Hat, which I'm sure attorneys have to wear quite a bit. Black Hat is looking at a situation's potentially negative outcomes. As attorneys you have to do this often; look at things cautiously and defensively. You have to think about why things might not work. It helps you be prepared.

As an attorney, when you put on this black hat, you have to realize when it is time to take it off and move on. I'm not going to say much more about the Black Hat because you are the experts on it; not me.

The next hat to talk about is the Green Hat; creativity. This hat emphasizes thinking about what's possible. You might ask yourself, "How can this grow? How can this improve? How can this move forward to the next step?"

This hat is pretty closely aligned with positivity, but it is more specifically about growing something versus a Pollyanna perspective.

For example, let's say you are a criminal defense attorney and your spouse is a family law attorney. You may look want to look at what kind of cases are bringing in the most money. Let's say, your average retainer is $2500 per case and your spouse charges a retainer of $6000 per case.

In terms of the Green Hat mindset, which one do you grow? If the goal is to make more money, perhaps there is a way you can help your spouse bring in more family law cases.

Or let's say maybe your partner is practicing criminal law and you see DUI is a waning opportunity, but misdemeanor drug cases are a growing opportunity due to an opiate epidemic. If that is the case, then you work on getting more drug cases.

The last way of thinking to discuss is the Blue Hat method, or organizational, process control. The Blue Hat is important because it manages the thinking process. It's the control of all of the other hats. It gives you a much more complete solution to your problem than just sitting there and saying I've got to think. I've got to figure this thing out.

Getting back to utilizing your competitors, again, the first way we talked about is to control your own emotions. That is not directly about the competitor. Rather it is about you.

The second we talked about was realizing what you can learn from these competitors.

The third way to make use of the competition is to act; do something. Don't just sit there angry at your business rivals. Don't just sit back and say, "Wow they do that really well. I wish I had done that."

Act.

Go get your website redesigned. Retrain your admin staff to do better screenings. Write a book on your practice area. Write two. Write three. Again, control your emotions. Learn what you can from competitors. Analyze that intel and then act on it.

I hope this discussion about how to use your competition to your advantage and the brief overview on the "Six Thinking Hats", has helped you. All of this has been incredibly helpful in my life and in my business. I hope it will be for you as well.

SPEAK-A-BOOK™ FOR ATTORNEYS (AN INTERVIEW WITH TRACY MERDA OF JACOBS & WHITEHALL)

Richard Jacobs: One of the most successful products we offer attorneys is the Speak A Book. It's a tremendous authority piece for legal professionals which allows them to stand apart from competitors.

There are many reasons why this has been an incredibly effective marketing tool for our clients, but I'm not going to spill the beans and spoil it for you.

Instead, I'm going to have Tracy Merda, our premier Speak-a-Book™ coordinator here at Jacobs & Whitehall, tell you more about it. She has been working with attorneys to create this product for a number of years now and has, in fact, overseen well over 200 Speak A Books in areas such as estate planning, DUI, criminal defense, auto accident, divorce, intellectual property law etc.

Tracy is well liked by our attorney Speak A Book authors, as she makes the process smooth and easy. Her goal is to help attorneys, who have wanted to write books for years, sometimes decades, write a professional, ethical and client attracting book in a very short period of time. I wanted to interview Tracy because she has an insider's look into the process and outcomes of the Speak A Books.

Tracy Merda: I've been working with attorney clients to create Speak A Books here at Jacobs & Whitehall for six, almost even seven years now. So yes, I have seen a lot going through our process and I've witnessed how it's evolved and changed throughout the years. I've worked with a lot of different attorneys and their goals shift and change over the years as well. It's definitely been an interesting ride. It's one of my passion projects that I get to participate in here at Jacobs & Whitehall. I'm really happy to talk about it.

Richard Jacobs: I've noticed you like it a lot. I've even tried to tempt you into other functions within the company, but you resisted because you love the book process so much. So, why do you like Speak-a-Book so much? Or do you love this process itself?

Tracy Merda: There are a few different reasons. I love it, for one, because I get to work with attorneys to create something that oftentimes, they have been dying to do or wanting to do for years.

I often hear the same story. They have been too busy and haven't had time to sit down and write a book or just don't know how to get their vision down on paper. It's one thing to think of a great book in your mind. I know I've probably thought of a thousand things I thought were great books for me to write, but for me to sit down and actually put pen to paper and draft that out, it would never happen. I think a lot of that happens with attorneys.

It's a lot of fun to see the excitement and success that my clients get to achieve when they actually do get the Speak-a-Book process finished. It's really amazing to them, and still to me, that it honestly takes just a few hours of their time to do this whole thing and create their masterpieces. I think it's phenomenal. I can't believe that this hasn't been an industry standard for the past 50 years. It blows my mind that we get to do this.

Richard Jacobs: Until probably 20 years ago, there was no such thing as desktop publishing. If you wanted to get anything printed, you had to go to a typesetter or a printer. People had very little control over anything that was printed. Then, desktop publishing came in and that allowed people to create, design, align and print things out on their own home printers. That revolutionized many industries.

About 10-15 years ago, the self-publishing world started opening up with Amazon. You could self-publish, it was becoming feasible, then easy to do, and more and more venues offered it.

Then, self-publishing became mainstream, and it freed people up to not only create their own books, but to publish them themselves on big platforms like Amazon, Kindle and Barnes and Noble, etc.

I think this is what changed the landscape to make it a million times easier than the authors of yesteryear to publish books.

Tracy Merda: Absolutely.

Richard Jacobs: What are some reasons attorneys tell you they want to author a practice-area book?

Tracy Merda: I think the reasons have evolved, even since I started working with Jacobs & Whitehall some years ago.

When I first started working with clients, a lot of attorneys seemed to want to do the books as an extension of their marketing. Over the years, and especially in the past probably year, our attorney clients (who are incredibly intelligent and very specialized), are looking not just to have a marketing piece, but to be an authority and set themselves apart from their competition in their metro and particular practice area.

The book topics have also evolved from being very general to more niched down and focused. For example, I just prepared an outline focused on representing non-US citizens who are facing legal challenges in the United States.

I've also done several books focused on specific topics within Intellectual Property, accidental death from vehicle accidents, and class action, drug-specific lawsuit books.

Those are not things that we would necessarily have been asked to do several years ago. Attorneys are smartly choosing much more niched down areas in which they want to project authority and expertise. I think that's a huge change for the better. Are you seeing that as well, Rich?

Richard Jacobs: Yes, and I think it's necessary because the old days of just putting out a generic profile doesn't work as well to stand out from competitors and attract new clients. I believe that's why we're seeing this niching, and that's where the money is. You can't compete effectively and earn a living being a generic attorney anymore, unless you niche your practice areas, at least a bit. So, I think that's why there's this push towards it.

Tracy Merda: It's almost like we have two different types of attorney clients that come to us to author books: One type is already an "expert" in their field or they're at the top of their game. They have had this idea of writing this book that they're going to use as a marketing piece, because it's a personal goal. I think that's a huge accomplishment in life and a great legacy to leave behind.

Then we have a second cohort of lawyers recently who have been in four or five different practice areas, and now want to niche down their focus and practice areas, to attract higher quality and higher paying cases and clients.

They are making a pivot or a change in their career to focus now from everything to just family law or just child custody cases, to narrow it down even further. Doing a book; and I have seen this work, is making them stand out from an SEO perspective, as well as in the general marketing scheme and by word of mouth referrals. It all comes down to really targeted marketing and narrowing practice areas or focus.

Richard Jacobs: What I also see is they're responding to how people look for attorneys, which nowadays is primarily through the Internet. Most attorneys understand the need for positive reviews and beautiful, compelling, content-rich websites, but there needs to be <u>more</u>.

Because searching the internet and having a presence there requires very little effort, and to look as good as the top firms requires only a medium-sized effort, lawyers must take it to the next level. There is where Speak-a-Book gives attorneys a competitive advantage, a demonstration of power, prestige, authority, and expertise, and sets them apart from their competitors.

Tracy Merda: Absolutely. It's a tool that can be used for so many different things. For example, the attorney can repurpose the content of the book on their website, in emails, and other places and that adds a lot of value to the whole process as well.

Richard Jacobs: How have you observed that the Speak-a-Book process has helped our attorney clients differentiate themselves in their marketplaces?

Tracy Merda: Many lawyers we work with in various practice areas tell me, "I have wanted to write a book for 5-10 years now. I want to come off as an expert, showcase professional stature, but I don't have the time to sit down and put pen to paper."

Authoring a book helps them get that edge, but it doesn't take months of work or years of effort. They avoid getting caught in the weeds of doing the actual writing by instead, doing a friendly 90-120 min recorded Q&A with me.

Richard Jacobs: Any particular anecdotes that attorneys have told you that really were eye opening for you and what the book did for them? Tell me some success stories.

Tracy Merda: One attorney I worked with was not well-known in his local area for practicing criminal law, which is something he wanted, but found it hard to include, because he was already known as the family law and personal injury guy in his metro.

Now he put out a book on criminal defense and started handing it out, promoting it on his website, showing it off at different speaking engagements, and giving it to other community members.

Slowly, then suddenly, his community and potential clients are seeing him more as a criminal law attorney, and he's attracting those type of cases.

It has allowed attorneys with those goals to grab that audience and those clients they want that maybe they wouldn't be able to without saying, "Consider me strongly for representation. I'm a published author and implied expert on this topic."

Richard Jacobs: Not only are multiple attorneys being called by potential clients and discarded at a moment's notice, but unfortunately, there is no shortage of cut-rate juniors that will "do it cheaper".

Attorneys I know really hate to deal with this, especially if they've been practicing for a good number of years and they know that they bring a lot more to the table than someone who has only been around for a few years. So, in terms of price resistance, if you have authored a book and you are up against someone who hasn't, how would that help you to win the business?

Tracy Merda: You now have the authority in your practice area. So, if I'm the potential client, I'm going to be willing to pay more for an attorney that I feel is highly qualified and is an expert in the arena.

When I do the actual interview with our speak-a-book clients, they want their prospective clients to be thinking,

"I want that ultimate professional is in this field. If he costs a little bit more; well, he's an author. His book is telling me that he is a smart guy. He is the authority in this field and knows what he is talking about." We talk about "Why hire this attorney? Why do I need an attorney? What do you bring to the table?" We can go into great detail on what it is that makes you the best in your business and the best in that particular practice area.

Richard Jacobs: The type of business attorneys are used to getting is referral business. That's the type of business that most attorneys, from my experience, prefer. Ideally, they want to get all referrals and not have to do this public marketing. That's a big distinction that the book allows them to get the type of clients they want from the sources they want; not just any client.

Tracy Merda: Yes, exactly. It can flush out some of the weaker prospects and those that really aren't going to go anywhere and the time wasters. Those aren't the clients that are hiring quality attorneys. They aren't someone who is willing to pay the big bucks or someone who will appreciate an author or an expert in their field. You're going to get better quality clients overall.

For one particular client, 99% of his business was referral already. When he decided to shift to just focusing on criminal law, his business was drying up because no one knew him for that. After the book was out, it was like wildfire. All of a sudden, he was the guy to go to for criminal matters.

I also had a discussion with another attorney recently who specializes in criminal defense for individuals who are in the United States but who are not citizens. For whatever reason, they have run into some sort of legal complication and he deals with getting them home and back and forth, etcetera. What he told me that I found interesting was that the clients he is looking for, he doesn't want to pick them up by putting his face on a bus bench. He didn't want to be on the billboards. Those are not clients who need what he does. He was absolutely right, because it's so niched down in such a specialized kind of law and practice, that he needed something like the Speak A Book to grab his audience. He needed something for potentials to have in hand, that would explain exactly what he can do for them.

You know, most people are not going to sit down and read the entire book, front to back. But once the potentials have it in hand, there it sits, as a reminder on a table or on a shelf. Some will pick it up and read it. Others will pass it on to a friend or colleague. Once the book is finished, he will be able to repurpose the content to his website. There will also be a widget on the site, where potentials can enter their contact info and get a copy of the book for free, and so on. All of these things that we do, including the book, all come full circle and they're all great to be used together.

Richard Jacobs: How else are people using their books?

Tracy Merda: I had one gentleman who was brilliant with how he promoted his book. He was handing it out in the dentists and doctors' offices, placing his book on their tables in their waiting rooms. I know that might be an old school, grassroots approach, but you'd be surprised how well it worked to get him clients.

Anyone that knows you've written a book, give them a few copies. Everybody knows somebody who needs an attorney. It's a great way to get your name out there as the authority and still flush out the bad seeds who just want free information. They aren't going to come back and bother you if they've already got it. Who cares? It's a PDF version. It's not going to cost you a thing.

But the referrals, that's really big and you should be sending it to old partners or old colleagues. There are so many ways that you can use all of the different versions of the book that we provide.

One of my favorite things to tell clients is that when you are finished with your book, whether you get the physical copies or not, it should be going out to every prospective client that calls. Your staff should be trained on what to say, what to do, extract contact information from the prospective, send out an email with the book attached, and so on.

If you have the physical copies, it should be the same thing. Your admin should be getting the contact info and mailing out hard copies to good prospects. I think this is huge, and it costs you practically nothing to do that. The same thing should be done if you're speaking at engagements or anything like that. Have copies on hand, hand them out, e-mail them out, do what needs done.

I think it's also important to use it on the website for repurposing content, creating video voiceovers with some of the content, and so on. There's just so many different things that you're getting with a Speak A Book. This book can be used in so many different ways and that's what I try and drill home to our clients.

Richard Jacobs: What about getting into the media? For some lawyers, that's vitally important to them. They would love to be quoted or called when something happens in the news, and they want to give their opinion on it. What opportunities would having a book present to you for being in the media?

Tracy Merda: Depending on your market, where you are, and on how big of a news day it is, if you have the appropriate marketing staff, you can put out press releases. You can have them say something like, "Attorney Smith, author of such and such, just published his latest book on," whatever it might be. Send it out to every news outlet you know. That costs you nothing but maybe a little bit of time.

Additionally, I know a lot of the attorneys that we have partnered with over the years are very high status, as far as their media connections. They have appeared on shows or radio stations. It just offers that level of prestige. If you didn't already have a media placement, maybe now they're going to take a second look at you because you are an author. If you already had the media placement, it adds some really great feathers in your cap to go out with your name.

Richard Jacobs: I had helped an attorney in Florida do a series of books for his firm. He did one on DUI and then he went to a local bail bondsman and gave him the book. They weren't allowed to say, "Hire this guy," but he gave them books and they had them on the desk so potentials could see it when they came in. People were picking them up and calling the attorney. So, he was getting some good business that way by working with some referral partners.

He also had a personal injury book on auto accidents. The same bondsman company worked with a number of body shops and brought books in to them to set around.

Tracy Merda: Absolutely! Those types of relationships with local businesses are really important.

One other thing, when you have the finished book, our clients get the book in every format you can dream of. So, you have the PDF version. You have the Word doc. You have all of these things. If there is a slight change in the law, or you want to change any of the content, you own this content; this is yours. Those things can be easily updated.

Right now, we are getting a lot of clients signing up for our Speak-a-Book Platinum package; where we are creating three different books from an existing book or a new book, by simply changing or adding a chapter in on another topic.

One example is a client that I worked with years ago came back to us, because he really loved a personal injury book we did for him. It was a general book on rear-end collisions. Now he wanted to create additional books from that original copy on head-on collisions, T-bone collisions and accidents resulting from distracted driving. Those are four similar, yet different topics.

What we did for him with this new service that we have is, we created separate chapters that were folded into his original material. We changed the covers and titles and some of the intro and concluding information. Lastly, we added in the new chapter and voila, we had three new books out of the one. Now he had four books, and was so ecstatic about getting these lined up in his office so prospective clients coming in would see this nice series that he'd done. I think it's a brilliant idea, it's so easy and we already have that relationship together. I already know what he wants and likes. It just makes it so much easier.

Give us one basic topic you want to focus on. Then we build three separate books out of that by simply adding in a chapter and making some cosmetic changes.

Richard Jacobs: The core of each book is the same and then there's an extra chapter that goes into a specific practice area subset. So, for instance for people that do DUI, you can create three separate chapters, each focused on second, third or fourth time DUIs and each can be a new book. You can have one based on DUI with a high BAC, or underage, a DUI with injury, etcetera. The same thing can be done for personal injury books, family law books and so on. There are a lot of different permutations of each practice area that you can use the same book or set of books to niche down and attract potential clients very specifically.

I call this the chicken soup for the attorney's soul method, aka Speak-a-Book Platinum. It works really well.

Tracy Merda: I think a bonus to this is that if you're a past client, we already have that rapport and relationship. I'm already familiar with your book. I'm going to go back and read it. We're going to get familiar with the content again.

If you're a new client and we're starting from scratch, we're doing the same kind of thing. We are going to create the core book and then we will blend these new chapters in with all of the rest of the material that we have. This is a very important project to me. I love the idea. I think it's amazing value for our clients.

Richard Jacobs: One thing people are always wondering is, will the Speak A Book work for any practice area and then what about Speak A Book platinum. Is there a practice area that you think this wouldn't work in?

Tracy Merda: I think the Speak A Book process works for any client who has the right mindset. One, you have to be willing to give me a couple hours of your time. It helps for clients who have a somewhat clear vision on a general practice area that they want to hit or what kind of business they need.

Also, the best book clients are generally those who are somewhat good with a simple deadline and if not, they are comfortable with a few nudges from me to get the necessary steps complete. Once they've done the interview with me, their hardest task and time commitment is pretty much over. From there, it's just a matter of signing off on the edits or proofs once they receive the manuscript. But again, it works best when the client is good about getting those things back to us in a timely matter and if not, they don't mind a follow-up or two from me. It really comes down to someone who wants to get the project done.

As far as topics go, it is completely open ended. I've done everything from really random IP law, where I had to do tons of research to even understand what we were talking about, all the way to general DUIs or car accidents. You can splice any practice area or topic at least three or four different ways. There is no practice area that is off limits as far as the Platinum Package or any Speak A Book goes, as far as I'm concerned. I don't see anything that we couldn't tackle. Maybe I'm missing something, but I haven't run across it yet.

Richard Jacobs: Attorneys know any practice area definitely has enough nuance and permutation in it that it could use at least one book on it if not multiple.

Tracy Merda: Absolutely. Again, look at the example we just talked about with the auto accident book being turned into four different versions. That is not even all of personal injury, of course. So again, every practice area can be broken down.

Richard Jacobs: The same can be said for family law, for example. There are divorces involving people who have kids and those without kids. There are -people divorcing after long term marriages and others who had brief relationships. There are people who want to divorce who own businesses versus where one or both spouses are self-employed and so on. Again, there are so many permutations in every practice area.

Tracy Merda: Exactly. For example, I just worked on a book for an attorney who focused solely on grandparents' rights. Every area can niche down for sure.

Richard Jacobs: What about the decision process? If an attorney is reading this and they do more than one practice area or even within a given practice area, how can they decide which one deserves a book first?

Tracy Merda: I had this conversation with an attorney the other day. He practiced two very different areas of law. He called one area his "moneymaker" or what he had to do; and then the other area of law was something that he more so dreamed of doing, his passion project cases that he really loved. After talking it through, I had to be frank with him. So I said, "What's more important right now? Do you need your bottom line met? Do you need to make money? Or do you want to focus on your passion?"

He said, "Well, I would love to do what I want to do, but I have to pay the bills first."

That was it. From there, we decided he was going to put aside the work he loved temporarily, and focus on making money first. The idea was to drum up business by doing this book to get the "moneymaker" cases and then he would come back and do a second book on what he really enjoyed talking about. A lot of people are already working mentally on a second book before the first one's even finished. That was his situation. Everyone's is different.

I always start with new clients by asking what kind of cases they want more of and what their goals are right now and with the book. If someone already has all the money and clients they need, then we say, "If you just want a book on your shelf with your name on it, that is fantastic. Let's do it. However, that's a different conversation and we may have a different method of getting there. If your primary objective is to get better and more clients, then let's focus on those cases first."

Richard Jacobs: Just like in that example, if you do multiple practice areas, maybe you pick the one that has the most competition in it and you really need to stand out, or you pick the area that makes you the most money. Everything becomes easier with good cash flow.

Tracy Merda: Right. With good cash flow comes extra time for you to focus on those practice areas that you don't have the time or bandwidth to do right now, because you need more revenue. All I can do is advise the Speak A Book client that, "From what you are saying to me, this is what it sounds like you should cover in the book."

It's up to them to decide if they want to focus on a general topic or if they want to niche it down further. I always recommend niching down, but if they want to cast a wider net, we can do that too. There's nothing that the Speak A Book process can't do. A lot of this comes from my relationship building with the client. Once we get that initial strategy session done, I oftentimes have a better sense of your personality, what your goals are, what your needs are, and then I can make my recommendations from there.

Richard Jacobs: What common questions do you get once attorneys sign on? Do they have any reservations? Do they have things that aren't obvious when they first contemplate doing this?

Tracy Merda: I think when a lot of attorneys start this journey or even before, they have this sense that this is going to be incredibly overwhelming. It sounds like such a big thing to do. I think a lot of people are relieved after we speak. I get that a lot. Attorneys are very nervous to start, some even up until the interview day. When I get them on the phone, they are saying things like, "I don't know how this is going to go. Am I saying the right things?"

When they're finished, there's always a very big sense of relief and they say, "So you're going to create this book for me out of what we just did?" And the answer is, "Yes. Absolutely. That's what the whole process is about."

I find there's certain things that work better for some attorneys versus others. For example, I have some attorneys who will probably over prep, as far as making notes underneath every question that I send them. Some practically write down the entire book and then speak to me on the phone what they have, and we fill in the blanks.

I have others who absolutely shoot from the hip because that's their best style; it comes very organically and natural to them. I always ask attorneys once I provide them with the outline and questions, "What is your natural speaking style when you're prepping for a presentation or speaking? Do you write everything out that you're going to say, or do you write notes?"

I work with clients within their own natural process to get them ready for the interview. It seems to go much smoother if we do it this way versus going against their natural tendencies. I think they're surprised at the flexibility of our program and how we customize the experience for everyone.

INDEX

NOTES